*To the memory of my sweet Westies, Meaghan and Caitlin,
who lovingly stayed by my side as I wrote this book.*

CONTENTS

All in the Mind

Body Language

Animalia

Relatively Speaking

Tomorrow Is Cancelled

A Metamorphosis of Darkness to Light

All in the Mind

Dancing through the Flames

Dancing through the flames,
 flesh seared,
  impotent to communicate
   his torment
    as the belt tightens around his neck.

He can't eat, can't sleep and is numb.
 Fed by others,
  he is told what to do and
   just like a child he is obedient.

He feels worthless and wants to die.
 They don't understand.
  He wants to die as he dances
   wildly through the flames.
    They burn, they burn, they burn
     as the belt tightens around his neck.

He doesn't feel complete.
 His accident robbed him of that.
  He does forgive –
   he just cannot forget.

A warm trickle runs down his leg
 and he does not know why.
  He is angry, then happy, then confused
   as the belt tightens around his neck.

Until one day when he is all alone
 in his sad, little room
  with no one to watch him
   dancing through the flames,

13

the belt is cinched
            through the last notch.
                        He turns blue.

He is found –
        barely alive.
                His future children
                        now have permission to exist.

But what about his soul –
        what happened to that?
                It lies trapped in limbo somewhere between
                        the accident, the belt and his dreams;
                                forever dancing through the flames.

Stream of Consciousness

speed
       ribbons of light
  impact
       froth   bubbles
s
i
n
k
i
n
g
     cold
   numbness
         silence...

thudding
        pounding
  rock against glass –
         a frantic
s – l – o – w   – m – o – t – i – o – n
     water ballet

windshield
     sha-tt-er-ing

   shards floating
       sinewy forearm
            oozing streams
    of red

consciousness
        unconsciousness
   consciousness –
     an awareness of

being pried
                                        from her coffin
        wrenched from
                        icy waters

saved by inches
                    and bitterly
        resentful
                        of her failed
        suicide

Gone

Gone –
the appreciation
of lake and jack pine,
reduced to vapid ghosts
of water and trees
reflected in tired eyes;

gone –
the psychic energy
sapped
by clenched muscles
and rushes of adrenalin
at the ring of a doorbell,
the creaking of pipes and
a furnace that speaks in tongues.

The remains –
a compulsion to examine
every nook and cranny
for monsters
lurking
in dusk's impending
darkness

in a house
bereft
of sunshine.

Anorexia

A skeleton
in the mirror
stares at a black
bathroom scale
on a white floor.

Obsession

Reach down into that dark place
and pull up a memory,
a nightmare,
an obsessive thought;
wrap it in wrapping paper
and re-gift it to yourself
over and over
in a frenzy
of self-flagellation.

Reach down into that dark place;
dredge up your demons
and have them devour you alive
with their gnashing fangs.

Dementia

aphasia

      agnosia

  apraxia

         aah aah

     keys in fridge

       lucid

            lucid not

      lucid

        lucid not

  grey matter

        metamorphosing

      into

  quicksilver

Furnace Filter

The furnace filter gags on dust,
eaves troughs choke on leaves and
the car thirsts for an oil change,

its indicator light winks unnoticed –
she hasn't driven after dark
for some time now

but she is acutely mindful
of having made it through another night
of shifting shadows and creaking noises.

She lies on her side of an empty bed
while the day looms large.
Reluctantly reaching for her slippers,

her brittle bones can't remember
whether she's taken her calcium pills.
She puts on yesterday's clothes

and wonders what in hell
she will do with the next
twenty-four hours.

The Elusive Language of Trees

The trees speak to me
                in tongues –
mortal that I am,
          incapable
                 of deciphering their messages
      nested
in the rustling of leaves and
            in the crepitation of branches
  whose outstretched arms
                are weary of supplication.

Like a type of aphasia,
          I am hindered
     by my mind –
the words of the trees rendered
                 unintelligible;
          I am impotent to commune
with that which beckons me

and in frustration,
           the trees become silent –
      their whispers lost
in the fresh stillness
              of the evening.

Body Language

|

A fading lilac	—	*H*	—	scar, flattened,
semi-inverted	—	*Y*	—	unlike its former self:
a purple vertical	—	*S*	—	speed bump
slowing traffic	—	*T*	—	in the vicinity
not as nasty as its	—	*E*	—	predecessor:
an abominable	—	*R*	—	abdominal
bloody gash	—	*E*	—	stapled
Frankenstein-style	—	*C*	—	barely binding
a precarious	—	*T*	—	chasm
of layers	—	*U*	—	of severed
flesh and	—	*M*	—	muscle;
organs	—	*M*	—	eviscerated
like a Thanksgiving	—	*Y*	—	turkey

|

I Brought Flowers to the Stroke Ward

but didn't know I wasn't supposed to;
just showed up with a bouquet –
glorious petals
in their glory
glory
morning glory
mourning glory

in her glory
before she had her shtro...chhhkk...uh
before she wasted away into
a garden gnome

held tilted downward
sitting immobile
in an off-limits
hospital bed

limited visitors –
visiteurs sans fleurs

no scents
stimulating or exciting
an already overstimulated
overexcited
bleeding
brain

I wasn't supposed to bring flowers
to the stroke ward
but I didn't know.
I didn't know.

Minuet in G(eneral Hospital)

Friday night in the emergency room –
my husband's moans of pain
in the throes
of a kidney stone attack.

To create some private space,
an ER nurse drew
a curtain that didn't quite touch the floor –
noisily sliding it along a semi-circular metal rod.

The IV drip was a welcome constant
in this sudden disorder
into which we were plunged –
a ripping away from our usual routine;

when the morphine began to take hold,
I happened to notice
the feet beneath the curtain –
the hems of tailored black slacks
above matching pantyhose and pumps,
standing next to another pair of feet –
a black sock on one foot; the other bare.

I could hear
their unintentionally loud voices,
but it was the feet that betrayed their deafness
as they glided towards each other
every time she spoke in his ear
and then moved away when she finished.

This lilting dance continued all night
despite the ugly sounds of pain
and the nurse's periodic visits;
the feet rhythmically swayed back and forth
reassuring in their graceful regularity
as they danced a Minuet in G(eneral Hospital).

Two Verses from the Waiting Room

I

Sitting in the reception area of the
Diagnostic Imaging Department,
I try to repress mental images
of a claustrophobic MRI machine
and its incessant jackhammering;
wasn't it only last year
that I was in this same place
waiting for him to have a CT Scan,
transfixed by the "Radiation Danger" sign
perched above heavy closed doors,
mesmerized by its red warning light
that blinked for the forty-five minutes
it took a radiology technician
to take x-rays of his brain –
Brain?
What brain?
You have a brain?
I used to tease;
apparently he does
and no one knows what is wrong with it.

II

At the hospital for yet another test –
diagnostics in an adjacent room,
the door is ajar and I catch a glimpse
of him lying on a narrow table with
electrodes taped to his scalp;
I strain to hear the technician's words,
anxious to snatch stray bits of information
but conversation is muffled by
a boom box whose music assaults
my left ear and forces
the right to do my bidding.
I want and don't want to be here;

I want to write a poem while I wait –
desperate for the comfort of my own words
but not having any paper on which to write them.
I catch glimpses of institutional-sized
laundry carts as they periodically lumber by
and I listen to spy codes over the intercom
as doctors are politely paged
to rush to the aid of the dying.

R$_x$

PHYSICIANS'
HANDWRITING,
THE   BANE
OF   EVERY
PHARMACIST'S
EXISTENCE,
IS A WOE
FULLY   MIS
UNDER   STOOD
PROTA   GONIST
IN THE   WORLD
OF PRE   SCRIP
TIONS   WHERE   il   leg
                  ible   pen
                  man   ship
                  causes
                  life   to
                  hang   in the
                  bal   ance

Dragon Haiku

chasing the dragon –
heroin addict's story
not a fairy tale

Yin and Yang

The Dr. Sun Yat-Sen
Classical Chinese Garden –

a harmonious interplay
of lily ponds, weathered rocks,
ornate trellises

and pavilion roofs
whose sweeping curvature
smile
upon winter-flowering plum,
cypress and bamboo –

imperial grace
in labyrinthine courtyards;
a unity of opposites,
a Taoist yin and yang.

Sanctuary
from the unchained dragon
down the block –

jade eyes flashing
as it swoops on bony wings

red reptilian scales
of spent syringes
and inverted bottles
bristling in a frenzy
to gorge
on the festering –

a threadbare trench coat
curled in the fetal position

matted hair
straggling out one end,

scab-encrusted feet
poking out the other,

yellowed claws
lined with strips
of dark green dirt

still clutching a bottle
next to a garbage bag
of empties

as the neighbourhood
struts, shuffles,
and staggers
around her;

battles for a shopping cart
laden with tawdry treasures,

furtive exchanges
of powdered promises
of escape,

prostitutes transacting
matters of the flesh
and addicts
who press their flesh
into shadowy nooks

only a needle's jab away
from sweet oblivion

on East Hastings Street.

Animalia

Marlin

A vertical matrix the color of brushed platinum,
rows and columns motionless but for fanning fins

interrupted by convulsive choreography –
sudden jerks that regroup flat silvery bodies

into a new array of communal fin fanning –
a syncopated tango that dances on until its rhythm is

s-h-a-t-t-e-r-e-d,
sabotaged by a blue torpedo hurtling forward

at one hundred kilometers an hour
frenetically stabbing the school

with its spear-like bill. Waters roil
in a marine ecosystem of life and death conflict

imperceptible at the sun-drenched teal surface
where trophy-seeking predators higher up the food chain

await their prey with bated breath and baited hooks
vying for a marlin to mount over their mantels.

Duckling

Condos tower over a wetland sanctuary
       where painted turtles sun themselves on flat rocks

    dragonfly helicopters
           dart among the reeds,
red-winged blackbirds alight
                swaying in the breeze;

damselflies skim the water
          for mosquito larvae and Daphnia,
      Canada Geese waddle imperiously along paths
next to the water
                glaring at passers-by

mallard drakes submerge their emerald green heads
      searching for minnows and algae,
           their feathered bottoms bobbing upright
        above the water.

A female mallard glides along the surface
      leaving a triangular wake of ripples
             that jostles her already-imprinted brood
         of downy ducklings
                swimming to the shore
       where she starts to peck at the runt

grabbing it by its nape with her bill

      and forcing its fuzzy head underwater

  again and again

despite the squawking of another female

    balancing diagonally on webbed feet

      flapping her wings in desperate protest

 against this infanticide –

an act so surreal

      that before it can even register

    in the minds of bystanders

         as more than spunky

maternal discipline,

the duckling floats

        limp

   on the water.

Convergence

The intersection
of a pane of sun and cloud
with a faint clink of hollow bones.
Bewildered black eyes.
Beak tipped with a droplet of scarlet.
Rattled.
Numbed.
A grounding paralysis
felling feathers
that once graced azure skies,
a grounding paralysis
and a fuzzy awareness
of the muffled patter
of mittened paws.

Anaconda

Twelve feet of serpentine muscle slither
across South American wetlands,
lying in wait for fish and baby caimans,
coiled, ready to pounce and mercilessly
constrict unsuspecting victims
under the blistering tropical sun.

The intense heat dries out its habitat
and even the anaconda must seek relief;
it is forced to slink through murky waters
which eventually evaporate
leaving only cracked clay cobblestones.

Body encrusted with dried mud,
scales lose their traction
rendering the snake immobile;
unable to escape, it slowly bakes.

The mighty anaconda heaves in agony,
reptilian head thrust backward,
gaping jaws raised towards the sky;
silent screams
rage against its earthen prison

in a defunct river,
formerly a sustainer of life,
now a parched wasteland
where a once-mighty predator
falls prey to the elements.

Lion on the Street

Dedicated to the animals that
perished in Zanesville OH

Magnificent beast –
regal ragged mane
tawny physique
muscles rippling
tail switching

fierce jaws opened wide
baring golden yellow spikes

menacing

       menaced

released from your ramshackle
chain link faux zoo –
a home-grown excuse
for an exotic animal

preserve

      an accidental abdication

your massive paws
unable to cloak the click-clack
of claws on concrete

your amber eyes
not wild for the gazelles
and wildebeest
of the Serengeti

but wild at the sight
of speeding metal
and rubber

wild at the sight
of your own blood
and guts

stripped of your majesty
stripped of your life

royalty relinquished –
just a lion
on the street

Copper

a fox kit
drowning
   awash in pus
   bloated abscess
   burgeoning
infection   spreading
 bone disintegrating
 ball and socket hip
dis   located

whisked
  from the wild
  to the sterile
 shaved
 rubber tube down throat
 death-mimicking anaesthesia

multiple surgeries
on stainless steel tabletops
   salty whimpers
   from a stainless steel cage

tentative return to wildlife center
   placed in a pen with
     vixen Cupcake
     foster mother of orphaned kits
     mentor of foxy ways
sly vixen
stealthy executioner
   her needle teeth
   lining determined jaws

 shake   shake   shaking   Copper

chunks of rusty fur missing
   tiny body convulsing
      then forever still

Escape

Piped-in elevator music,
       barely audible,
              wafts through a darkened room
       full of cages
where luminous green orbs
       reflect the scant light;
             even the dogs
       have refrained from yelping –
they whimper in their sleep
       while their feet twitch
             as they chase imaginary rabbits.

       Motionless but for her tail
swishing back and forth,
       she continues to stare
             with a look calculated to project
       laser beams that zap and vaporize
metal bars;
       their dematerialization,
             liberation
       recapturing the essence
of all that is feline
       as she slinks into the obscurity
             of the night.

Death Watch

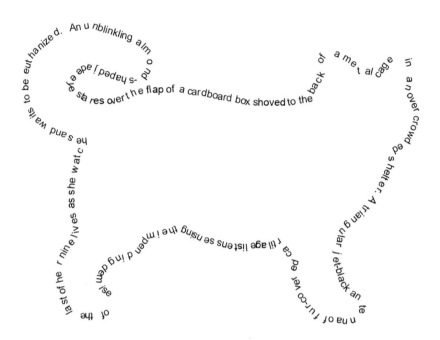

An unblinkling almond-shaped jade eye stares over the flap of a cardboard box shoved to the back of a metal cage in an overcrowded shelter. A triangular jet-black antenna of fur-covered cartilage listens sensing the impending demise of the last of her nine lives as she watches and waits to be euthanized.

Smoky

The dog's organs were
literally fried, according to
the vet who performed
the autopsy; his latex-gloved
hands barely able to touch
the insides of the burning
corpse – the intense heat
resulting from seizure after
seizure for at least thirty
minutes before death.

Found next to the rigid body,
a half-eaten smoky
spiked with white crystals –
strychnine
that would never
have been noticed by the
enthusiastic puppy who
loved to bark at his neighbour.

Alive in Death

For Caitlin

Sitting on the carpet,
I inhale deeply and reach out
to touch a yellow stain;
my arm goes rigid
as my hand splays fingers –
an electrical jolt
to my brain,
triggering anything,
any sense that reminds me
you are still here
even though your ashes
and empty collar
tell me otherwise,
tell me you are dead
and I can no longer feel you,
touch you or cuddle you.
All I can do is selfishly hope
your lingering scent
will never dissipate
even if it is a slight to your dignity
(I am so sorry)
because I need to know
I share a part of you that is tangible,
alive, and still with me
even in death.

The Ache of Time

For Meaghan

I carry the shape of my grief
over the dull ache of time –
her essence
always present.

I clutch,
grasp for her,
the tips of my fingers

just out of reach

as I try to hold on
to a life
that is physically
no more

as I try to cradle her,
to feel her breath on my face,
to know she is alive,
to feel her life,
to feel her love.

Relatively Speaking

My Father's Fingers

The Dirty Thirties. Two
rough and tumble brothers
chop, chop, chopped
wood –
their every breath
a ghost
in the winter air

as they chop, chop, chopped
wood
for a home warmed by
twelve children,
not coal.
A home
reduced to ten
by the mathematics of
loss,

scars of many variants
running deep
and sharp
especially for
the brother who
steadied a log
on a misshapen
stump
of a tree

a split second before
the eager blade of an axe
left its bloody wake
of severed
fingers, fingers, fingers
and a misshapen
stump
of a hand.

Somnus Erat Demonstrandum

Transitive Property of Equality:
If a = b and b = c, then a = c.

Lessons learned from parents –
a string of pearls,
wisdom
passed on from generation
to generation,
dispensing one bead at a time
lest we become overwhelmed.

Therefore, if wisdom comes with age
and age before beauty,
then wisdom comes before beauty
(sleep):
The Transitive Property of
Parental Reason.
S.E.D. (*Somnus Erat Demonstrandum*)

Carpe diem vs. beauty sleep:
to slumber or not to slumber –
"Don't sleep your life away",
my father's dictum
still haunts me with its irony;
having died prematurely,
he now sleeps his life away.

What Is a Mother

What is a mother?
Scan the shelves of a greeting card store
for clichés and trite comments about
a mother's love –
platitudes about her always being there for you,
for helping you to grow into the person
she is; the person you want to be.
Look for the largest, fanciest card
you can find –
hell, look at the bottom corner
on the back of every card to find
the most expensive ones;
read every saccharine verse,
every maudlin thought
and realize that despite their mawkishness,
these sentiments are legitimate –
your mother is one of the most
important people in your life
and before you know it,
she will be dead.

Lost

My son
is brimming with regret;
I look upon him
with such sorrow –

he is troubled and penniless,
lost and

alone

always on the

                           precipice.

I've consoled him
but he hasn't heard me;
his sadness
is a knife in my heart.

Have compassion
for his darkness.

Empty Nest

No wet towels
on the bathroom floor,
bed still made – unrumpled,
a few stray clothes
left hanging in the closet
not tossed onto the carpet,
no dirty dishes
on the kitchen counter
or in the sink,
none of his friends
coming to visit –
lots of food
in the fridge;
quiet.

I miss him.

Twin

Identical twins.
Ginger-haired,
freckled,
a twinkle in their eyes
as they each pretend
to be
the other –
two halves of a
whole,

one half
stalked by leukemia –
purple bruises creeping
leopard-like
over his body,
snarling as they drag
their kill away.

Vigilant. His brother
watches
and waits
for his turn.

It never comes

burying him
in guilt
every time he
passes
a mirror –
a living reflection
of the child
his parents
lost.

Tomorrow Is Cancelled

Return to Sender

Neither snow nor rain nor heat nor gloom of night stays these
couriers from the swift completion of their appointed rounds.
Inscription on the General Post Office, New York City

No snow, no rain, no heat, no gloom of night –
just good old-fashioned sunshine enveloped

the mail truck as it dog-ged-ly
grappled its way to the summit

passing conifers and homes nudged
slightly askew by their mountain host

on a glorious Disney morning –
flowers a-bloomin' and birds a-tweetin'.

The postmistress steered her van with one hand
while she sorted mail with the other,

experienced eyes darting back and forth –
road, mail, road, mail, road, mail

until the road got lost in the mail
and she found herself being returned to sender,

truck plummeting into the azure lake below.
A splash. Silence. Eternity....

Now she is but an anecdote stamped into memory –
local folklore shared with tourists on lazy summer days.

The Barber's Daughter

It happened thirty years ago
but I still remember every detail –
I was helping my dad in our corner grocery store
when the door flew open,
"Come quick! There's been a terrible accident!"

Snip, snip go the shears at the barbershop.

"Ray was riding his motorcycle!
He wasn't speeding!
The kid ran from out of nowhere!"

Clippings from the haircut quietly drift to the floor.

"She ran out from between parked cars!
Her mom couldn't catch her!
Geez, the kid was only four years old."

The customer admires his haircut in the mirror.

"The woman is hysterical...
Oh my God, the father doesn't know yet!
He's still at work!"

Sweep, sweep, sweep the hair.

While customers huddle around my dad's counter,
listening to the grisly tale of a toddler's life
splattered all over the street,

a dustpan falls to the floor.

I didn't see the barber or his wife for a very long time.
When I finally did, their dull faces were worn
and full of loss,
How could it possibly be otherwise?

Mourning Mist Haiku

ghosts of morning mist
hover above still waters
overturned canoe

Not Yet

Altogether too many
funerals –
fists clutching
wadded-up tissues,
streaks of mascara
fleeing from red eyes,
the stifled sobs
of halting eulogies.

Too many inhabitants
of pine boxes –
the *others*, never us.

Not yet.

Too soon to undertake
our rendezvous
with eternity –
it's not our turn,
perhaps soon,
soon enough.

Not yet.

Why Are the Dead So Still

Arms crossed, lying motionless
in an open casket,
he gazes upward through closed eyelids.
Maybe if I look hard enough
I'll see him flinch or wriggle his nose
at the acrid smell of incense
rising from the censer;
holy water is sprinkled on his body –
it tickles, so why doesn't he laugh?

Proudly dressed in his finery,
he's unaware of us as we mill past
to say our final goodbyes;
we stare at his waxen appearance,
wondering when our turn will come
and whisper kind comments to which
we rudely receive no response –
death is a stubborn master,
it compels complete passivity.

We are told that he is at peace,
that he has attained eternal happiness –
not a physical happiness surely,
he can't even laugh anymore.
When the casket is closed
and he is laid to rest,
he's unable to breathe a sigh of relief
punctuating a lifetime of pain
because the dead must be still –
that is the rule.

Corpse

Clumps of earth
land with hollow thuds
on a pine lid
surrounded by six-foot
planed walls of earthen clay;

inside, the body,
a corpse weeks before –
bedridden,
head tilted backwards
with gaping mouth
and beak-like nose –

a spent bird of prey
poised for the last time,
ready to snatch death
in its dulled talons,

the raptor's stealth
foiled by its stertorous breath
and yellowed eyeballs
rolled back in their sockets

as family gathers round
watching,
waiting.

A Funeral in the Rain

Under a slate-coloured sky,
raindrops pelt umbrellas
balanced on long legs –
flamingo-like
above weary heads;

silent tears blend with the rain
and trickle onto the drenched grass.

All else is quiet
except for the drone
of a prayer for the deceased
and the occasional whoosh
of a distant car
splashing through puddles,
oblivious to the grief
of those who mourn.

As the service concludes,
some linger
in the rain-soaked cemetery
to pay their respects to loved ones
who have long since passed on
to their final resting place –

a place where it doesn't matter
why the bereaved weep,
for the deceased or for themselves –
a grim reminder
of their own mortality.

They shed tears
that subside like the rain
as the clouds pass
and those above ground
depart
to resume their daily routine.

She Lives inside My Lungs

Ashes to ashes, dust to dust
Book of Common Prayer, 1662

I watch her bone-white ash
scattered on the wind
drifting
floating

her cremated remains
free

to settle on weeping willows
to skim lake waters
and to live

as particulate matter
inside my lungs

Liminality

Liminality

                 transience

           undefined borders

      where the spume of salty swells

meets sandy shores

          surf meeting sand

sand meeting surf

      where footprints of the soul

soon disappear

much like the life they possess –

liminality

           transience

Who Will Weep for Me

When the sun finally sets
and I draw my last breath,
who will weep for me?
After I have passed on,
the physical gone –
bereft of reality,
let my spirit rise
and serve as my eyes
so I may know
who wept for me.

Shiva Call

Spat from the belly of a hearse
like Jonah's unceremonious exit from the whale –
not left to drown, but drowning nevertheless
as visitors file in and out
to humbly pay their respects.

They come with casseroles in hand
and hugs that echo through my hollowness –
self-conscious expressions of sympathy,
well-intentioned diversions
from the darkness residing within.

* *Shiva* – a Jewish custom to visit the bereaved

electronics

room
  black
   as midnight sky
but for pinpoint
stars –
        green
        bluish-white
        red
LED dots
linked
by imaginary lines –
        constellations
        pricking holes in the night
like the memories
        of my dead
  friend

Dare Not Disturb the Periwinkle

'Tis bad fortune to remove the periwinkle from a graveyard,
for ye shall vex the spirits dwelling therein.

                                                    Folklore

Dare not disturb the periwinkle,
the myrtle that creeps
across barren sod
'twixt granite headstones
above the caskets
of the corpses below.

Dare not disturb
the inviolate –
a sacrilege worthy of
the wrath of the shades
who haunt these
hallowed grounds.

Dare not disturb
their shrouds woven
from the graveyard vine
whose flowers are as blue
as the lips of the dead.
Dare not disturb the periwinkle.

Noche tras noche

Noche tras noche
en el silencio
de mi cama,
cuando las paredes
reflejan las sombras
de los árboles bailando
sensualmente
en la luz de la luna,
pienso en las almas
que susurran sus secretos
tratando de explicar
su existencia espectral,
frustrados –
los muertos
sin palabras.

Night After Night

Night after night
in the silence
of my bed,
when the walls
reflect the shadows
of trees dancing
sensuously
in the moonlight,
I think of the souls
who whisper their secrets
trying to explain
their spectral existence,
frustrated –
the dead
without words.

A Metamorphosis of Darkness to Light

In the Beginning

Silence, then from the void, cosmic chaos –
atoms belch across a universe
pulsating with Mephisthophelean
fury of infinite proportion,
colliding in a drama of fire and brimstone,
coalescing into a primaeval plasma soup
from which the embryonic stuff of life
creeps onto cooling shores
instinctively replicating,
evolving into erudite, sophisticated
beings learned in technology,
brashly overconfident and dangerous,
desecrating and vilifying the sacrosanct,
flinging matter into infinity and
strewing stars into oblivion.

Butterflies

In the dark void, the beast awakens
and snarls.
Obsessed by dreams of unspeakable evil
perpetrated upon the butterflies
beyond his nether world,
he lusts to rip them apart –
silken wings hanging in tatters
from his drooling jaws.

Butterflies flutter around him
perversely attracted by his spell,
unable to break free.
Incapable of flitting,
fleeing or flying away,
they are forced to witness their species
quiver and perish
in the gaping maw of the beast.

oil spill

viscous
black
ooze
meanders
downstream
siphoned
into
the
ecosystem
suffocating
the
life
from
all
flora
and
fauna
in
its
wake
silently
assaulting
the
environment –
strangulation
by
oily
fingers –
a
legacy
of
sinister
stains
and
a
grim
reminder

**of
human
carelessness**

Night

The night is edgy
        sexy
     a cover for back room deals
          and clandestine exchanges under
     the yellow glow of sodium street lamps;
  an unsettled time
             when dark masks light –
     a time for lovers and thieves,
        of dreams and
  strays
          prowling along alleyways
and caterwauling
     under the stars.

Metamorphosis

Night melts into morning –
a gentle metamorphosis
of darkness to light
seeping through chinks of time
to transform one world
into another.

Sapphire Seas

Inky swells heave –
the rhythmic breathing
of sapphire seas
crested with
flashes
of gold
as the sun sinks
below the horizon
and drowns the waters
in darkness.

Shadows on the Wall

Muted light – diffuse and grey,
slinking through spaces
between venetian blinds
casting crisp shadows on the wall:
horizontal stripes hiding behind
a dracaena's silhouette –
angular leaves and twisted trunk;
the reflection of a martini glass –
its inverted liquid triangle
glowing momentarily
with magnified intensity
then fading with the shadows.

Reflections of Infinity

At opposing ends of a corridor,
two mirrors confront each other
in a contest of wills
stubbornly flinging images
into infinity –
a cycle of reincarnation
animating the essence
of reflected light.

Lake Winnipeg

Furious crests surge, billow and pummel the shore,
Spewing spray like a geyser from a whale's blowhole,
Foamy grey waves crash with a deafening roar,
As they ebb and they flow and they pitch and they roll.

Surly leaden clouds surrender muted beams of light,
Revealing a barely discernable pinpoint adrift,
Spied by weary seagulls buffeted by winds in midflight,
It's a fisherman bravely casting a net from his skiff.

Sailboats docked in the marina, bob upon the lake,
Masts rhythmically rising and falling in sync,
Nestled alongside the boardwalk sheltered from the wake,
With only the breakwater separating them from the brink.

Cool Jazz

A curl of thin blue smoke
snakes around a half empty glass
of stale scotch
and as the ice cubes melt,

the lazy swooshing of a brush
caresses percussion cymbals,
the mellow plucking
of thick strings on the double bass

in counterpoint with the twang of an electric guitar
and the pained expression on the guitarist's face;
while sultry saxophone romances the house,
confident fingers fly across the keyboard –

pianist, eyes closed, sways back and forth
entranced by the rhythm he creates,
shoulders heaving as he makes love to the piano –
it's jazz and it's cool baby; uh huh.

A Blind Man Describes Red

Teach me red, said the blind man;
describe red to me.

Certainly.
Red is a cherry,
a stop sign, ketchup ....

No, no, said the blind man,
that is not the essence of red.
I will describe red to you –

Red is palpable –
it is the flush of passion
in a lover's breast,

the convulsive fury
of a charging bull,
the bite of jalapeño
on the tongue;

red is the fiery radiance
of tropical summers

and red is the cosmic life force
pumping through us all.

That is red.
That is the red you do not see
but I do,
said the blind man.

Angels Beat Thy Wings

Angels beat thy wings; descend to earth
    With the power of legions
Of armour-plated warriors forging into battle;
    Triumphant trumpet flourishes shall herald thy coming –
Majestic harbingers of power, glory and grace.

Descend

Descend

Descend

Enlighten us with thy radiance –
    Animate our souls with thy splendor;
Illuminate this sojourn – our earthly passage,
    Imbue us with clarity of vision.
Angels beat thy wings; descend to earth.

conception

a spray of letters and syllables
coalesce into droplets of words –
iridescent sounds tinkle
trickling into an ephemeral pool
of stanza and verse

Magic

And for his next trick –
abracadabra!
He pulls a rabbit
out of his
proverbial hat
charming the ladies,
not with his prestidigitation
but with the magic
of his smile.

Neruda on the Beach at Capri

A trembling sun drips
beads of molten gold
onto disc-shaped pebbles
washed smooth by the surf
that ebbs and flows
with the sensual rhythms
of love-making,
sea foam caressing
the feet of a man
adored by all women –
romanced by his
red velvet words;
Madre Chile's exile,
he strolls along
the beach at Capri,
surrounded by cliffs
that dwarf him –
he is a towering giant.

Morning Rapture

The stillness of morning stirs
and spills quiet light
displacing last night's gloom;
I stretch and purr
basking in the velvety softness
of yesterday's sleep,
diaphragm rhythmically heaving.
The sun streams through windows
blanketing me with its radiance –
an energizing rebirth
even for the padded paws
scrambling to greet me
with sloppy kisses
and welcome a new day.
The morning is timid and peaceful –
an intimate solitude not to be shared
with those who sleep.

I Touch a Singing Ghost

I touch a singing ghost –
the essence
of the eternal
that thrums
in a voice
resonating
with the musicality
of stars –

crystalline,
pure,
piercing.

My fingertips
reach out
grasping at
the impalpable,
the ethereal,

the essence
of the eternal.
I touch a singing ghost.

I Am

I am the stars,
the wind, a crystal,
a blade of grass,
a feather.
I am entropy –
a random assortment
of oxygen, carbon,
hydrogen, nitrogen
and trace elements
in a body
that happens to exist
at this point in time,
its individuality
organically interconnected
to the universal;
I am a body that possesses
limited cognition –
an integral
but trivial speck
of infinity.
I am a part of the universe.
I am the universe.
I exist. I am.

Acknowledgements

Special Thanks

A very special thank you to New Westminster Poet Laureate Emerita, Candice James at Silver Bow Publishing, not only for helping to bring this project to fruition, but for her expertise and thoughtfulness.

Credits

The poem, "I Am", was selected as Poem of the Month for Canada by the former Canadian Parliamentary Poet Laureate, Pierre DesRuisseaux, and is featured on the Parliament of Canada website.

"I Am" was also showcased online in *The Globe and Mail* in conjunction with a feature article about Fern G. Z. Carr.

The English version of this poem and Carr's Italian translation, "Io sono", won an international poetry contest in Italy – *Concorso "Il Meleto di Guido Gozzano"*. Both versions were published and read at an awards ceremony there. Her Spanish translation, "Yo soy", was published by the University of Wisconsin in *zona de carga*.

The poem, "Cool Jazz", was nominated for a Pushcart Prize by *The Worcester Review*.

Other poems in this book were first published in Australia, Austria, Canada, Finland, India, Israel, Mexico, New Zealand, Peru, Romania, Seychelles, Singapore and the USA in:

Ars Medica; *The Art of Music*; *The Body Electric*; *Bones II*; *Caesura*; *The Café Review*; *Carbon Culture Review*; *Chrysanthemum*; *Cirque*; *Contemporary Poetry*; *Danse Macabre*; *dirtcakes*; *disorder*; *The Effects of Grace*; *Eunoia Review*; *Green's Magazine*; *Jewish Women's Literary Annual*; *The Language of Dragons*; *Longest Hours*; *Memory and Loss*; *Metric Conversions*; *Miracle*; *Okanagan Arts*; *Outlook*; *Pasque Petals*; *Paws, Claws, Wings and Things*; *Petals in the Pan*; *Poeming Pigeons*; *Poesía y Opinión*; *Poetry New Zealand*; *Poetry*

USA; *Scarlet Leaf Review*; *Sipay*; *Skive*; *SOL*; *Soliloquies Anthology*; *Talvipäivänseisaus Special*; *Voices Israel Group of Poets in English*; and *White Wall Review*.

Poems from this book have been broadcast on *P.I. New Poetry, Poetry Super Highway Blog Talk Radio*, and the Public Lending Right Commission's podcast for National Poetry Month. They have also appeared online as well as being featured on blogs by the League of Canadian Poets.

"conception" was included in a University of Alberta and Edmonton International Airport Wave Interactive Media Installation.

"Furnace Filter" was one of Carr's poems in *Bones II* that won an Editor's Choice Award.

"Noche tras noche / Night after Night" was composed and translated by the poet herself.